IMPEACHMENT: A HANDBOOK

IMPEACHMENT

A HANDBOOK

Charles L. Black, Jr.

Yale University Press
New Haven and London

Designed by Sally Sullivan and set in
Times Roman type. Printed in the
United States of America.

ISBN 0-300-07954-0 (cloth)
ISBN 0-300-07950-8 (paper)

Library of Congress Catalog Card Number: 74-82692

A catalogue record for this book is available from the British Library.

The paper in this book meets the guidelines for permanence
and durability of the Committee on Production
Guidelines for Book Longevity of the
Council on Library Resources.

10   9   8   7   6   5   4

To my sister,
Betty Black Hatchett,
with much love

Contents

Foreword by Akhil Reed Amar   ix

Preface   xv

1. INTRODUCTION   1

2. THE PROCEDURES   5
General   5
The Part of the House of Representatives   6
The Part of the Senate   9
Some Special Procedural Points   14
    Is Impeachment, with Trial thereon, a
       "Criminal Proceeding"?   14
    Should Hearings be Public?   19
    Is There Any "Presidential Privilege" in
       Impeachment Proceedings?   20
The Final Responsibility of Congress   23
The Place of Lawyers   24

3. THE IMPEACHABLE OFFENSE   25
"Treason"   25
"Bribery"   26
"Other high Crimes and Misdemeanors"   27
The Relation between Impeachable Offenses and
    Ordinary Crimes   33
An Affirmative Approach to the Meaning of
    "high Crimes and Misdemeanors"   36

Application to Particular Problems   41
  Bribery   41
  Income-Tax Fraud   41
  Use of Tax System to Harass Opponents   42
  *Impoundment of Appropriated Funds for the
    Purpose of Destroying Authorized Programs*   42
  Unauthorized Warlike Operations   44
  Improper Campaign Tactics   45
  Obstruction of Justice   45
Some Final Considerations   46
  *The President's Responsibility for Acts of his
    Subordinates*   46
  Good-faith Belief in the Rightness of an Act   47
  Substantiality   48
A Note on History   49

4. IMPEACHMENT AND THE COURTS   53
Is There to be Judicial Review of the Senate's
  Verdict on Impeachment?   53
May Congress Use the Federal Courts to Assist
  in Impeachment Investigations?   53

5. SHORT   OF IMPEACHMENT   65

Appendix A: Bibliography   71

Appendix B   77

Foreword

When Charles Black wrote this little big book on presidential impeachment, Richard Nixon was in the White House but (we now know) on his way out. As I write this foreword, Bill Clinton is in the White House, and no one can be sure what tomorrow will bring. What we can be sure of is this: most of the wise words of this small yet great book are as apt today as they were a quarter-century ago, during the last impeachment crisis. And I suspect that this book's wisdom will remain apt, whatever President Clinton's ultimate fate, whenever the issue of presidential impeachment next grips the nation, whether in 1999, or 2020, or . . .

This is no coincidence. For Black's genius was to rise above the partisanship and petty politics of the day—to reflect on the underlying and enduring questions of constitutional law that apply equally to Republicans and Democrats, conservatives and liberals. In this book, written for citizens and lawmakers rather than judges and law professors, one of the most surefooted constitutional scholars of the twentieth century takes lay readers on a grand tour of the constitutional issues raised by presidential impeachment, pointing out the major pitfalls and landmarks in this treacherous terrain.

Black does not try to give us all the right answers. No

(good) guide could, because many of the answers must come from ourselves. In true Socratic spirit, Black often gives us the right questions to ask ourselves, and helps us see why certain answers are wrong, leaving to us the burden of choice among the set of plausible answers that remain. The right question to ask, says Black, is not "what are the finite set of offenses that James Madison had in his head when he agreed to the phrase 'high crimes and misdemeanors'?" but rather, "what misdeeds do we today—here and now—deem so gross and malignant as to warrant undoing a national election?" And any answer that is tinged by partisanship, Black suggests, must be wrong. The impeachment process is not merely about replacing a leader who is at present sagging in the polls or whose party has lost its majority in Congress. Rather, it is about punishment and dishonor— permanently banishing from political office someone who has done deep wrong to the country. Precisely because we should oust partisan thoughts from our mind during impeachment, Black's analysis as applied to current (or future) events may be even better than today's (or tomorrow's) op-eds. Black's most vivid hypotheticals—involving, believe it or not, young White House interns, pot smoking, and immoral sex—were not written to save or to undo Bill Clinton, or whoever next has his (or her) neck stretched across the constitutional chopping block. Black's words are cool, not hot—and they can teach things we may not learn elsewhere.

Impeachment: A Handbook is a perfect marriage of author and topic, for the issues of presidential impeachment are powerfully framed by a mode of constitutional analysis that is Charles Black's trademark, his signature. In turn, this approach—which Black calls "structural" interpretation—is perhaps nowhere more powerfully deployed than on the issues addressed here. Consider the phrase "high crimes and misdemeanors." A constitutional textualist might say that whatever this phrase means, it should be the same for lower federal judges and cabinet officers on the one hand and for presidents on the other. But structurally, this makes little sense. When a lower federal judge or cabinet head is impeached and removed, the nation undergoes no great trauma. No federal judge or cabinet secretary has a personal mandate from the national electorate, and so her removal does not undo the votes of millions. Thus, to a Blackian structuralist, what counts as a sufficiently "high" crime must be read against the backdrop of other parts of the Constitution, which make clear that presidents are very different from other officers. (Analogously, the Senate has always accorded more deference to the president's nominations for cabinet offices than to his nominations for Supreme Court posts. Although the same phrase— "advice and consent"—applies to both, there are obvious structural differences between the two. Cabinet officers are part of the president's team and will leave when he leaves. Supreme Court justices are not and will not, and so the president is structurally entitled to less deference when he nominates justices who will be in place for life.)

Thus one of Black's most important conclusions derives from the basic structure of the Constitution, and indeed is built into the basic structure of this handbook: this is a book about *presidential* impeachments, because these are constitutionally unique.

Another important conclusion that Black deduces from the very structure of the Constitution is this: final judgment in presidential impeachment is given to the Senate, sitting as a High Court of Impeachment, and no appeal of any sort may lie from this court's judgment to the Supreme Court or any other ordinary court. Other like-minded constitutional scholars might be tempted to argue for this conclusion by pointing to constitutional case law, or text, or history—and Black does make some important textual and historical points. But his fundamental argument is structural: it would simply make no structural sense for judges to try to reinstate an ousted president. The basic architecture of our system of government, its central structures of legitimacy, must doom all efforts to appeal the judgment of the High Court of Presidential Impeachment, whose findings of fact and law must stand as *res judicata* in all other tribunals.

And this conclusion—that the constitutional decisions in this field are to be made by senators and representatives on behalf of the citizenry, rather than by law-trained and erudite Article III judges—in turn must influence the proper style of constitutional exegesis. What is called for in analyzing impeachment issues is not a web of technical lawyering that weaves together detailed historical expositions for the benefit of judges steeped in intricate doctrine. Rather, proper analysis of impeachment issues requires a plain, short statement of what is at stake, and what makes good sense, constitutionally. This is what Black gives us by example.

As to these issues of substance and style, and many others, Black's book seems every bit as persuasive today as the day he wrote it. As to one set of issues, however, the world may have changed dramatically in ways that invite rethinking his conclusions. When Black wrote this book, C-SPAN did not cover Congress as a matter of course, and Court TV did not regularly beam trials into our living rooms. The internet did not exist. These new technologies raise hard questions about how much of the impeachment process should be immediately accessible to those of us who live outside the Beltway, and how much, in turn, those inside the Beltway should listen to well-informed sentiment in the hinterlands. On the one hand, Black is surely right to be concerned about trial by polls and media circuses. On the other, how much legitimacy is there in a process that is open to those who live within commuting distance of the Capitol, but not to the rest of us?

These questions should remind us that this book cannot save us from deciding many hard issues raised by our own times in our own times. Charles Black, I am sure, would want it no other way.

Akhil Reed Amar
Southmayd Professor of Law
Yale University

Preface

My thanks go to Chester Kerr and to all at the Yale University Press, for extraordinary help and cooperation—but most especially to Jane Isay, the best of editors; to Margaret Abelson, for expert and most timely typing help; to Eileen Quinn, both for that and for valuable suggestions on the manuscript; to the staff of the Yale Law School Library; to Barbara Aronstein Black, for ideas developed in many discussions while the book was germinating, and for several crucial suggestions toward the end. On all public law matters, as in so many other ways, I have benefitted through the years from the works and friendship of Max Gluckman, whose constitutional studies of the Barotse, and of other societies remote from our own, have concentrated in great part on the eternal problems of removal and succession; luckily, he and Mary Gluckman have been in New Haven while this book was being written. I never can publish anything in constitutional law without acknowledging afresh my pervasive debt to Alexander Bickel, for what are now eighteen years of generously given access to his rich store of knowledge and thought.

Vade libelle!

C.L.B., JR.

New Haven
May 21, 1974

1. Introduction

For the first time in more than a century, and for the second time in our history, the country has in 1974 been faced with the live possibility that a president may, in the words of the Constitution, "be removed from Office on Impeachment for, and Conviction of, Treason, Bribery, or other high Crimes and Misdemeanors."

The presidency is a prime symbol of our national unity. The election of the president (with his alternate, the vice-president) is the only political act that we perform together as a nation; voting in the presidential election is certainly the political choice most significant to the American people, and most closely attended to by them. No matter, then, can be of higher political importance than our considering whether, in any given instance, this act of choice is to be undone, and the chosen president dismissed from office in disgrace. Everyone must shrink from this most drastic of measures.

Yet the Framers of our Constitution very clearly envisaged the occasional necessity of this awful step, and laid down a procedure and standards for its being taken. Their actions on this matter were, as the records of their debates show, very carefully considered. As is true, however, of most other parts of their Constitution, they put in place only a very general framework, leaving it to the future to fill in details, and leaving many questions open to honest difference of opinion. This book is about the procedure and standards set up by the Constitution, and about some of the questions that must still be answered. While all civil officers of the United States, including federal judges, may be impeached, this book centers on presidential impeachment.

When one is writing, as an academic constitutional lawyer, for laymen, on debatable questions of law, one ought perhaps to confess one's biases, so that allowance may be made for these. I should say first that, both in voting and in published writing, I have from my youth quite consistently opposed the president who has been the subject of recent proceedings—except for my having taken the public position, at an early stage in the deplorable train of events leading to those proceedings, that he (or any president) ought to be held to enjoy an ample privilege of confidentiality as to communications with his own staff in the White House, and that, to put it concretely, he was under no obligation to give up the celebrated tapes—a position that enjoyed little support from others. To countervail (as I hope) my lifelong political set against just about all of this president's positions, I confess to a very strong sense of the dreadfulness of the step of removal, of the deep wounding such a step must inflict on the country, and thus approach it as one would approach high-risk major surgery, to be resorted to only when the rightness of diagnosis and treatment is sure.

The Framers of the Constitution have left us, as they must, a legacy not only of certainties but of questions. Where the answer to one of these questions seems to me clear, I shall state and endeavor to support my own position, sometimes trying to state also the arguments for the contrary view. Where, as must often be true, I look on a question as more or less open, I shall so treat it, trying to give arguments on both sides. An understanding of the questions is more important than a fixed conviction concerning the answers.

This book is for the citizen. What part ought the citizen to play in the process of impeachment and removal? My own answer would be that, for the most part, our attitude as to any impeachment ought to be that of vigilant waiting. The impeachment process, whether "judicial," "nonjudicial," "criminal," or "noncriminal," resembles the judicial criminal procedure in that it is confided by the Constitution to responsible tribunals—the House of Representatives and the Senate—and in that these bodies are duty-bound to act on their own views of the law and the facts, as free as may be of partisan political motives and pressures. In this process, a snow of telegrams ought to play no part.

At the same time we cannot, and perhaps ought not try to, keep ourselves free of opinions concerning the process; such views inevitably form themselves as one tries to follow and understand what is going on. In their formation, we ought to try to take the same stance of principled political neutrality that we hope to see taken by the House and the Senate as they go about their work. This is not easy, particularly as to questions that have no certain answers; it is always tempting to

resolve such questions in favor of the immediate political result that is palatable to us, for one never can
definitely be proved wrong, and so one is free to allow
one's prejudices to assume the guise of reason. The
best way to combat this tendency is to ask ourselves
whether we would have answered the same question
the same way if it came up with respect to a president
toward whom we felt oppositely from the way we feel
toward the president threatened with removal.

One further point: it is the cardinal principle at least
of American constitutional interpretation that the Constitution is to be interpreted so as to be workable and
reasonable. This principle does not collide with respect
for the "intent of the Framers," because their tran-
scendent intent was to build just such a Constitution.
American constitutional law, as expounded by judges
and others, is full of instances of the application of this
principle. Applying it to doubtful questions regarding
impeachment, in this book for the laity, I shall give
chief emphasis to arguments of a practical cast. Such
arguments do not have the fine savor of ancient learning, but they are the ones that usually do prevail in our
constitutional law, particularly when it is at its admired
best; and they have the advantage that laymen can
understand them—in itself not an inconsiderable merit
when one is dealing with a constitution meant for all.

For those who wish to pursue any aspect of the subject further, the Bibliography in Appendix A, taken
from a recently issued public document, opens every
road. The constitutional provisions relevant to impeachment and referred to in the text are gathered in
Appendix B.

2. The Procedures

General

The procedures of the House of Representatives and of the Senate are highly technical, but most of this technicality is irrelevant to essential understanding. Let us consider in broad outline the processes of impeachment and removal.

Strictly speaking, "impeachment" means "accusation" or "charge." The House of Representatives has, under the Constitution, the "sole Power of Impeachment"—that is to say, the power to bring *charges* of the commission of one or more impeachable offenses. These charges are conventionally called "Articles of Impeachment." The House "impeaches" by simple majority vote of those present.

The Senate "tries" all impeachments—it determines, on evidence presented, whether the charge in each Article of Impeachment is true, and whether, if the charge is true, the acts that are proven constitute an impeachable offense. Such an affirmative finding is called a "conviction" on the Article of Impeachment being voted upon. A two-thirds majority of the senators present is necessary for conviction.

This two-stage procedure was borrowed from the British model (impeachment by the House of Com-

mons and trial and conviction by the House of Lords).
It is also analogous, obviously, to the two stages in
traditional English and American criminal law—"indictment" (or charge) by the grand jury, and "trial"
by another jury. The "Articles of Impeachment" cor-
respond to the *counts* in an indictment presented by a
grand jury. The Senate's vote on individual Articles,
one by one, corresponds to the trial jury's separate
verdict on each count of an indictment. This two-stage
procedure has obvious merits, in criminal practice and
in impeachments. It assures consideration of the evidence by more than one body, and screens out (at the
first stage) insubstantial or clearly unprovable accusations, so that the public and private trouble and ex-
pense of a full trial are avoided, in all instances where
the first or "charging" body—in the case of impeachment, the House of Representatives—finds nothing
worthy of full-dress treatment.

The Part of the House of Representatives

Let us now take a more detailed look at procedure
in the House of Representatives. Although the Constitution does not require it, the House has always employed one of its committees (usually the Judiciary
Committee) to investigate and report on charges that
might lead to impeachment; in the presidential case in
our times, several resolutions seeking impeachment
were referred to the Judiciary Committee for full investigation and recommendation. In only one instance
in our history has impeachment ever been voted by the

House of Representatives without an affirmative committee recommendation.

The committee to which this task is confided must hear evidence—great masses of it in a complicated case. At this stage it seems certain that no technical "rules of evidence" apply. (Indeed, I shall argue later that they do not apply even in the Senate trial.) Evidence may come from investigations by committee staff, from grand jury matter made available to the committee, or from any other source. Testimony before the committee, and the production of documents or other objects, may be compelled by subpoena—which is an order for appearance, or production, under the threat of criminal penalty. In addition to evidentiary matters, the committee must also consider whether the acts shown probably to have been committed are "impeachable" within the meaning of the constitutional text (of which much more will be said in Chapter 3). What part is to be played at this stage by lawyers of the person under investigation would seem to rest in the sound discretion of the committee. Where the committee concludes, on the facts and on the law, that one or more impeachable offenses are shown with sufficient clarity to justify trial, the committee reports, to the full House of Representatives, its recommendation that one or more "Articles of Impeachment" be adopted.

When this recommendation reaches the full House, it might conceivably be amended, but this is politically unlikely. It is just possible that the House might vote to *drop* one or more Articles of Impeachment, but next to impossible that any would be added, because an Article added against the recommendation of the committee that had heard all the evidence would stand on dubious ground in the Senate and in the country. The House will almost certainly not hear any more evidence but will vote, after debate, on the question whether to impeach or not, voting on all Articles of Impeachment together or on each separately. As a variation on this procedure, the committee may generally recommend impeachment, and if the House votes to follow this recommendation, the matter would be referred back to the committee, for the drafting of Articles; these would then have to be voted on by the whole House.

An affirmative vote by the House sends the Bill of Impeachment, with one or more Articles, to the Senate for trial—just as a grand jury indictment, with one or more "counts," goes to the trial court and jury, for final determination of guilt or innocence.

A majority of the House of Representatives (218 members out of the 435) constitutes a "quorum," so that, with a majority present, business can be transacted. Since a vote of impeachment is by simple majority of those present, Articles of Impeachment might theoretically be voted by one-fourth plus one of the full membership. In fact, it is unlikely that many members would ever absent themselves from the vote on a presidential impeachment. Such an absence would be hard to explain to constituents.

One thing that both the committee and the House leadership will try to avoid is a close vote along party lines—a vote whereby Republicans and Democrats divide as such. An impeachment voted that way would go to the Senate tainted, or at least suspicious, and would be unlikely to satisfy the country, because party motives would be suspected. This desire for bipartisan backing will expectably result in there existing some leverage on the part of the minority members of the committee and of the House—in our times the Republican members. In other words, some compromise will be sought which can win the adherence of at least a fair number of them.

The final role of the House of Representatives is to appoint "managers" to present in the Senate the case for conviction and removal on the Articles of Impeachment. The House, in effect, is the prosecuting party at the Senate trial, and the managers are the House's counsel.

Managers may be chosen either by general ballot on names in the House of Representatives, by passage of a resolution containing a complete list of names, or by a House-passed authorization to the Speaker of the House (its presiding officer) to appoint managers. These managers are congressmen, but they will be assisted by staff—probably drawn from Judiciary Committee staff. Generally, both political parties are represented, but no one would (for obvious reasons) be likely to be made a manager who had not supported the impeachment resolution.

The Part of the Senate

Upon receipt of Articles of Impeachment voted by the House, the Senate must resolve itself into a tribunal for trial. Where the president is accused, the chief justice of the United States presides; in this case, as in the trial of all impeachments, the senators take a special

oath (over and above their oaths of office) to "do im-
partial justice according to the Constitution and laws."
Both these circumstances give emphasis to the fact that
the Senate—whether for this occasion you call it a
"judicial" body or not—is taking on quite a different
role from its normal legislative one.

Many other factors, indeed, lead to the conclusion
that the Senate's function in impeachments is to be seen
as much like that of a judicial court; whether it really
"is" such a court is a sterile question of nomenclature.
Until a very late stage in the Constitutional Convention
of 1787, all drafts of the Constitution provided for trial
of impeachments by the Supreme Court; when this was
changed to trial by the Senate, there was no hint of any
changed conception as to the *nature* of the function or,
much more importantly, as to the proprieties of its exercise. The Constitution says, in Article III (the Judiciary Article), that "the trial of all Crimes, except in
Cases of Impeachment, shall be by Jury . . ."; the implication is that the impeachment trial is a "trial" much
like others, except that a jury is not to be used. The
special oath which senators take has already been mentioned. The Senate is to "try" all impeachments, not
simply vote on them; the word "try" is a word used
almost invariably in regard to judicial trials. Political
good sense points the same way; a judicial or quasi-
judicial trial is simply one that inquires into the facts
and the law, without partisan or narrow political bias,
and proceeds to judgment accordingly—these things
are obviously what we want in impeachment proceedings. In function, then, the "trial" in the Senate is, as its
name implies, at least quasi-judicial. The important

thing is not the name given but the thing desired—total impartiality, at least resembling that of a faithful judge or juror.

Here a difficulty arises—one which can be solved only by great and self-insightful integrity. It must almost always be the case that many senators find themselves either definitely friendly or definitely inimical to the president. In an ordinary judicial trial, persons in such a position would of course be disqualified to act, whether as judges or as jurors. It cannot have been the intention of the Framers that this rule apply in impeachments, for its application would be absurd; a great many senators would inevitably be disqualified by it, and it might easily happen that trial would be by a quite small remnant of the Senate. The remedy has to be in the conscience of each senator, who ought to realize the danger and try as far as possible to divest himself of all prejudice. I see no reason why this cannot produce a satisfactory result.

Members of the House of Representatives ought also, in acting on impeachment, to try for the impartiality of a good grand-jury member; I have reserved the point to the Senate stage because it is a more critical and crucial one when the final trial is at hand.

On special oath, then, and under the chief justice as presiding officer, the Senate begins to hear evidence on each of the Articles of Impeachment. The case for conviction will be presented by the managers for the House of Representatives; the president will be represented by counsel, but may appear in person, as does the defendant at a criminal trial, though this may be dispensed with by the Senate at the president's request.

Each side will call witnesses and introduce docu-
mentary evidence, bearing on the issues framed by the
Articles of Impeachment. On any procedural question,
including admissibility of evidence, the chief justice
will make a ruling, but that ruling may be reversed by a
majority vote of the senators present. After all evidence
is in, argument will take place.

The Standing Rules of the Senate provide that there
may be appointed a "Committee of Twelve" to hear
evidence in the trial of impeachment and to report to
the full Senate; "twelve" must be borrowed from the
jury system. This provision is of dubious constitutionality, in view of the language confiding to "the Senate,"
and not to some part of the Senate, the "sole Power to
try all Impeachments." It seems unlikely that such a
procedure would be followed in the trial of a president,
where it is essential that absolute bedrock legitimacy
be inarguably present—and where the business of the
trial is the most important business, by far, to which
any senator could be attending.

After all evidence and argument have been heard,
the Senate must vote. The vote is separate on each
Article of Impeachment. If no Article registers a two-
thirds vote for conviction, a judgment of acquittal is
pronounced and recorded. If one or more Articles of
Impeachment receive a vote of two-thirds or more, then
the president is convicted, and judgment of conviction
and removal is pronounced by the chief justice.

The Constitution says that the impeached officer
"shall be removed" on conviction of "Treason, Bribery,
or other high Crimes or Misdemeanors." There may be
a question whether this language is absolutely manda-

tory, with no possibility of distinctly lesser action, such as reprimand. It may be that some power of mercy or leniency is to be read into any such language by implication, unless expressly excluded. But the question is not at all likely to arise in a presidential case; if there were a disposition to leniency, this disposition would almost certainly take the form of an aborting of the process at a much earlier stage. Politically, the country could not live with a president actually convicted of "Treason, Bribery, or other high Crimes and Misdemeanors." It seems to be optional with the Senate whether to impose the additional penalty of disqualification from office. No "further" punishment of any kind may be imposed, though the removed officer, including an ex-president, may later be tried and punished in the ordinary courts, for the very offenses that were grounds of removal.

In voting on each Article of Impeachment, each senator, acting in a capacity combining those of judge and jury, is registering his best judgment "on the facts" and "on the law." This means that he is answering two questions together: "Did the president do what he is charged in this Article with having done?" "If he did, did that action constitute an impeachable offense within the meaning of the constitutional phrase?"

It might be emphasized, finally, that the senator's role is solely one of acting on the accusations (Articles of Impeachment) voted by the House of Representatives. The Senate cannot lawfully find the president guilty of something not charged by the House, any more than a trial jury can find a defendant guilty of something not charged in the indictment. This follows from elementary principles of fair notice, as well as from the linkage implied by the constitutional phrase, " . . . on Impeachment for, and Conviction of . . . " It could hardly make sense to read this as allowing impeachment for one thing and conviction for another. As an obvious corollary, Senate acquittal is not an endorsement of the president, or even an approval of his conduct, but only establishes that the senators voting in the negative were unconvinced of his guilt on the actual Articles of Impeachment brought in by the House of Representatives.

Of course, any material uncovered in the course of a Senate trial might be matter for a new impeachment in the House of Representatives. But the cumbersomeness of this, as well as its political unlikelihood, makes it highly desirable that the House be very careful to draw its Articles so as to charge offenses that can be proved, and that are likely to be held impeachable by the Senate.

Some Special Procedural Points

Is Impeachment, with Trial thereon, a "Criminal Proceeding"?

The president is impeachable for "Treason, Bribery, and other high Crimes and Misdemeanors." Treason is a crime. Bribery is a crime. It would seem that a "high Crime" must in some sense be a crime. What about a "misdemeanor" or "high misdemeanor"? It seems unlikely that such a phrase, in such a string, abruptly changes the subject. Nevertheless, some have contended that impeachment, and Senate trial, are not criminal proceedings at all.

The best thing to say about this question is that it need never have been asked in general form. It makes no difference whether we *call* impeachment a "criminal" proceeding or not, any more than it makes any difference whether we *call* it a "judicial" proceeding or not. What does make a difference is ascertaining those things in the impeachment process that should be treated *like* the same things in a criminal trial, and what things need not be. On this question, or set of questions, much can usefully be said.

Let us take first the question of proper attitude toward the *facts,* and toward the problems of *proof,* and of *burden of proof.* As a simple, and typical, factual question, let us take, "Did the president, on a given day, and at a given time, say 'X' or 'Y'?"

Now in a civil, noncriminal trial, say, an automobile accident case, if some witnesses testify that "X" was said, and others testify that "Y" was said, the juryman or judge must decide whom to believe, and if he finds slightly more credible the testimony of the "X" witnesses, he "finds" that "X" was said. The usual noncriminal rule is that the facts are determined by mere "preponderance of the evidence," as that preponderance registers with the judge or jury.

In a criminal case, on the other hand, guilt must be established "beyond a reasonable doubt." In the example I have given, if there were no very clear or cogent reason for believing one witness or set of witnesses over another, the duty of the trier of fact would probably be to find for the defendant, since mere conflicting

testimony, with no clearcut and weighty reason for believing either side, creates a doubt that cannot usually
be said to be "unreasonable."

Of course the example I have given is almost un-
realistically simple. A more realistic issue of fact might
be, for example: "Did the official on trial perform an
action *because* a campaign contribution was given, or
was this a coincidence?" Either is possible; the "finding" of this "fact"—the "fact" of corrupt or blameless
motivation—may entail the drawing of complicated
inferences from circumstances; the circumstances
themselves may be proven with more or less clarity.
Before the "fact" can be "found," the trier of fact must
decide on a standard of proof. Should he find an impeached president guilty of corruption if it seems
slightly more likely than not that a corrupt motive was
present? Or should a finding of guilt have to rest, as in
a criminal trial, on evidence which leaves no "reasonable doubt"? It makes a big difference, as the example
I have just given shows.

Nor is the matter quite this simple, for there are
intermediate rules in between the "mere preponderance" rule and the "reasonable doubt" rule. As to some
questions in some civil cases, for example, "clear and
convincing" evidence is required—something *more*
than a mere 51% "preponderance" of evidence, but
something *less* than evidence leaving no room for reasonable doubt. What is the right standard for judging
guilt in an impeachment proceeding?

Of course we don't know the answer with any sure-
ness; we have to work it out for ourselves. As with so
many constitutional questions, we have to ask what is

reasonable, and the reply is here far from obvious. Removal by conviction on impeachment is a stunning penalty, the ruin of a life. Even more important, it unseats the person the people have deliberately chosen for the office. The adoption of a lenient standard of proof could mean that this punishment, and this frustration of popular will, could occur even though substantial doubt of guilt remained. On the other hand, the high "criminal" standard of proof could mean, in practice, that a man could remain president whom every member of the Senate believed to be guilty of corruption, just because his guilt was not shown "beyond a reasonable doubt." Neither result is good; law is often like that.

Of course each Senator must find his own standard in his own conscience, as advised by reflection. The essential thing is that no part whatever be played by the natural human tendency to think the worst of a person of whom one generally disapproves, and the verbalization of a high standard of proof may serve as a constant reminder of this. Weighing the factors, I would be sure that one ought not to be satisfied, or anything near satisfied, with the mere "preponderance" of an ordinary civil trial, but perhaps must be satisfied with something a little less than the "beyond reasonable doubt" standard of the ordinary criminal trial, in the full literal meaning of that standard. "Overwhelming preponderance of the evidence" comes perhaps as close as present legal language can to denoting the desired standard. A unique rule, not yet named by law, may find itself, in the terrible seriousness of a great case. Senators have no plainly authoritative guide in this matter, and ought not to be censured for the rule they conscientiously choose to act upon, after thought and counsel, and above all in total awareness of the dangers of partisanship or feelings of distaste.

Another question, concealed by the question whether impeachment is a "criminal" matter—or even a judicial matter—is "What rules as to the admissibility of evidence ought to be enforced?" In an ordinary trial, for example, we exclude what we call "hearsay" evidence —testimony by one witness that another person, not a witness, told the witness that something had happened. We exclude evidence of the defendant's character, unless he himself seeks affirmatively to establish his good character. And so on through a considerable range of technicality.

Here, I think, the sensible answer comes clear. These technical rules of evidence were elaborated primarily to hold *juries* within narrow limits. They have no place in the impeachment process. Both the House and the Senate ought to hear and consider *all* evidence which seems relevant, without regard to technical rules. Senators are in any case continually exposed to "hearsay" evidence; they cannot be sequestered and kept away from newspapers, like a jury. If they cannot be trusted to weigh evidence, appropriately discounting for all the factors of unreliability that have led to our keeping some evidence away from juries, then they are not in any way up to the job, and "rules of evidence" will not help.

A third question concealed in the question whether impeachment is "criminal" has to do with the *law*. It is a cardinal principle of Western justice that criminal punishment ought not to be visited on anyone without clear warning of the criminality of his acts. It cannot be said that the phrase "high Crimes and Misdemeanors" has the clarity we would require of an ordinary criminal statute. Yet it is the phrase the Framers gave us; in the next chapter we will try to resolve some of the issues concerning it, though not all are tractable to resolution. At this stage, perhaps, all we can say is that a conscientious senator ought to insist upon being quite clearly convinced that the impeached official knew or should have known the charged act was wrong, before he votes for conviction. This simple rule should resolve many difficulties.

Should Hearings Be Public?

There may be early stages in the investigation process in the House when confidentiality should be maintained. Public disclosure of raw evidence, not yet evaluated as to credibility or relevance, might do some harm, and can do no good. In the later stages, and certainly in the Senate trial, it seems to me that the proceedings should be just as open as those in any courtroom. With reporters present, and with members of the public coming and going in the galleries, all danger of substantial secrecy would vanish. Trial on an impeachment is public business.

I would on the other hand (though I am certain that others will disagree) most strenuously advocate that radio, television, and cameras have no more place in this solemn business than they have in any other trial, and for the same reasons. There is no point in inflicting humiliation greater than that inflicted by the mere fact of impeachment. Nothing solid is added to public information by making a continuing spectacle of a trial. Above all, television, radio, and photography *act* upon that which they purport to *observe*; what one sees and hears is not what would have occurred if these modern means of communication were not there. At least there is a great danger of this, a danger often realized in the past, and that is enough to justify exclusion.

Continual nationwide television exposure contains another danger: it maximizes the chances of development of public pressure for some given result. It is of course the duty of senators not to take such pressure into account, but we would regard as totally unfair any other sort of trial where such pressure was applied. It therefore seems wrong to encourage it. The judgment of the public ought to come after the fact, on sober and long consideration of a record which will remain accessible forever. Play-by-play coverage contributes in no way to the formation of this ultimate evaluation, the only one that counts. The taking, at intervals, of public opinion polls on guilt or innocence, should be looked on as an unspeakable indecency.

Is There Any "Presidential Privilege" in Impeachment Proceedings?

Early in the investigations leading to the commencement of the latest presidential impeachment process, the president claimed the privilege of withholding from other branches of government the tenor and content of his own conversations with his close advisors in the White House. I regarded this claim as moderate and reasonable, and thought its upholding was essential to the efficacious and dignified conduct of the presidency and to the free flow of candid advice to the president. There was little public agreement with the view I then expressed, and the lower courts, though granting some scope to the privilege, took a very narrow view of it. I hope the question can be reconsidered in quieter days; I do not desire to unsay anything I have said. As time went on, however, the factual situation changed. The president himself released copious quantities of what I would have regarded as privileged material. Further, the issue, for purposes of the impeachment process, is not whether any federal or state court, or any committee of Congress, can force revelation of the president's conversations with his close advisers, but whether that can lawfully be done by a House committee conducting an impeachment investigation, or by the Senate at an impeachment trial.

As to the effect of the release of some material by the president, I wholly reject the theory that the president "waives" his privilege of confidentiality by releasing some material as to which the privilege might have been claimed. The enforcement of this "waiver" seems to me wholly wrongheaded, for it must make any president reluctant to reveal anything, for fear he will be held to have "waived" his privilege altogether.

As to whether and at what stage the privilege (if it exists at all) becomes invalid in an impeachment proceeding, I stand in some doubt, and can do no more for the reader than open the issues.

To begin, it seems that the privilege has a stronger claim in the earlier stages of the impeachment process than in the later. An investigation in its earlier stages may often be rather diffuse, and the close relevance of any given material may be correspondingly less obvious. By the time of the Senate trial, it should be much more sharply clear what bearing any particular matter has on the issues as now precisely drawn.

Further, one must distinguish between two quite different reasons underlying claims of presidential confidentiality. First, it may be claimed that *particular substantive information* cannot be divulged without harm to some vital national interest—predominantly national security. Secondly, it may be claimed that, regardless of the sensitive character of the substantive information, disclosure of conversations will impede the processes of consultation in the White House, since participants must always feel on parade, if they know that revelation of what they say can easily be compelled by any committee of Congress or by a court, and their perhaps tentative positions then publicized.

The second of these reasons may not be good enough to defeat the claim of the Senate (to take the strongest case) to the information it needs in an impeachment trial. It seems inevitable that the first reason—substantive national security—still has room for operation, even at that level. Suppose, for example, that a president were to be charged, in Articles of Impeachment, with having dangerously denuded the United States of its defenses, on some occasion of international tension. That charge could not be plumbed without delving into the most secret aspects of the military establishment—including, it might be, data on the deployment and capacity of our nuclear submarines. I should think that, in such a case, it might well be the plain duty of the president to decline to furnish this information at a trial, where its dissemination could not adequately be controlled.

In sum, my own views on presidential privilege are not now the received ones, and as a practical matter it seems unlikely that the Houses of Congress will concede the privilege much scope in an impeachment proceeding. But a temporary wide agreement on such issues does not authoritatively settle them; a presidential claim of privilege might therefore still be made in good faith. If it were made, some of the questions just explored would become relevant.

The Final Responsibility of Congress

We are used to confiding (or to imagining we confide) all constitutional questions to the courts. I shall later maintain that "judicial review" has no part to play in impeachment proceedings. For now, it should be briefly pointed out that, if I am right, then Congress, in acting on the matters just discussed and on those to be discussed in the next chapter, rests under the very heavy responsibility of determining finally some of the weightiest of constitutional questions, as well as a great many important and difficult questions of procedure. For this purpose, and in this context, we have to divest ourselves of the common misconception that constitutionality is discussable or determinable only in the courts, and that anything is constitutional which a court cannot or will not overturn. We ought to understand, as most senators and congressmen understand, that Congress's responsibility to preserve the forms and the precepts of the

Constitution is greater, rather than less, when the judicial forum is unavailable, as it sometimes must be.

The Place of Lawyers

Impeachment is a matter of law, foursquare and all the way, and lawyers must run the process, as surely as doctors must run the operating room. The Congress can get plenty of lawyers, and the money to pay them with. The position of the president is more problematic. Some may think that it is wrong for public funds to go to the financing of the defense of an impeached president, or of one threatened with impeachment. Yet, if we turn the question around and look at it from another side, do we want the outcome of this most important of proceedings ever to be affected by the president's lack of adequate legal help?

We must understand, also, that the participating lawyers are *advocates,* whose job is to take a side and present it with skill and vigor. Our entire legal system bets a great deal on the proposition that this "adversary" system is the least imperfect way to develop all the truth; the corollary is that we must look on partisanship not as an evil but as a part of the system's working. No one, including the president, can be treated lawfully if he is not adequately represented by counsel committed to him. Intemperate public attacks on lawyers, for the positions they take as advocates, are really attacks on our adversary system of justice. Such attacks are particularly surprising when mounted by other lawyers while legal proceedings are pending.

3. The Impeachable Offense

We come now to the heart of the matter. What offenses are impeachable? The constitutional categories are "Treason, Bribery, and other high Crimes and Misdemeanors."

"Treason"

Here we are on smooth ground. The Constitution narrowly defines "treason," in Article III:

> Treason against the United States shall consist only in levying War against them, or in adhering to their Enemies, giving them Aid and Comfort.

There is, in short, no reason to think the word means anything other than this in the impeachment passage. This makes irrelevant a great deal of learning (interesting enough in itself) about treasons under English law, except insofar (and that is not very far) as the contemplation of these throws light on the interpretation of the exceedingly narrow American definition. Since the situation in our times has in no way implicated "treason," the subject may be put to one side.

"Bribery"

The first point to be made here is that bribery may mean the *taking* as well as the *giving* of a bribe. At the Constitutional Convention, Gouverneur Morris gave the instance of Charles II, who "was bribed by Louis XIV."

As to both the taking and giving of bribes, several cases that have lately been in the spotlight remind us that the *states of mind* of giver and of recipient are all-important. There is nothing wrong with receiving a campaign contribution from dairy interests; there is nothing wrong in raising the price-support on milk. The question is as to the connection between the two events. An old English judge said that "The Devil himself knoweth not the heart of a man." But courts have to try, and continually do try, to work out the truth about intents and motives, for these are often (in bribery cases as elsewhere) of the very essence of the charge.

Is it "bribery" (or attempted "bribery") to suggest to a federal judge, engaged in trying a case crucial to the executive branch, that the directorship of the Federal Bureau of Investigation might be available? It is not wrong to offer a good district judge an important job. Almost all district judges, almost always, have government cases pending before them, in some number. Again, it is *motive* or *intent* that is crucial and that is hard to prove.

Careful, patient inquiry into and weighing of the facts is essential before one even begins to judge, in cases such as these. Beyond doubt, such cases are suspicious, but suspicion is not enough. On the other hand, it is not always a hopeless task, though it is usually a very difficult one, to establish improper motives on circumstantial evidence. In cases such as those here used as examples, there is nothing a conscientious congressman or senator can do but to suspend judgment until all the evidence is heard and analyzed.

"Other high Crimes and Misdemeanors"

This is the third, catchall phrase in the formula designating impeachable offenses. The reader will hardly need to be told that it must generate, and has generated, great difficulties of interpretation. Some definite things can be said about its extent, but we will be left with an area of considerable vagueness. Let us take the definite things first.

It would be well to start with the one and only discussion of the phrase at the 1787 Constitutional Convention. The day was September 8, 1787, just nine days before the Constitution was signed and transmitted for the adherence of the states. The impeachment provision, as reported out by the last of the convention committees (except the final one charged only with polishing the style of the Constitution), listed "treason and bribery" as the only grounds for impeachment and removal. The colloquy we need to look at was brief, taking perhaps five minutes:

> The clause referring to the Senate, the trial of impeachments agst. the President, for Treason & bribery, was taken up.

Col. Mason.   Why is the provision restrained to
Treason & bribery only? Treason as defined in the
Constitution will not reach many great and dangerous offences. Hastings is not guilty of Treason.
Attempts to subvert the Constitution may not be
Treason as above defined— As bills of attainder
which have saved the British Constitution are for-
bidden, it is the more necessary to extend: the power
of impeachments. He movd. to add after "bribery"
"or maladministration". Mr. Gerry seconded him—

Mr Madison   So vague a term will be equivalent
to a tenure during pleasure of the Senate.

Mr Govr Morris, it will not be put in force & can
do no harm—   An election of every four years will
prevent maladministration.

Col. Mason withdrew "maladministration" & sub-
stitutes "other high crimes & misdemeanors" <agst.
the State">

On the question thus altered

N. H— ay. Mas. ay— Ct. ay. (N. J. no) Pa no.
Del. no. Md ay. Va. ay. N. C. ay. S. C. ay.* Geo. ay.
[Ayes—8; noes—3.]

This is by far the most important piece of evidence
on the original intention with regard to the "other high
Crimes and Misdemeanors" phrase. It is true that the
proceedings of the Convention were secret (a fact, like
the fact that the Supreme Court deliberates in deep
secrecy, not often mentioned by those who would have
us think that secrecy in public affairs is always wrong).
But the men present were representative of their time,
and their understanding, at the moment when the cru-

cial language was under closest examination, tells us a great deal about its meaning.

It is interesting first that this passage quite definitely establishes that "maladministration" was distinctly *rejected* as a ground for impeachment. The conscious and deliberate character of this rejection is accentuated by the fact that a good many state constitutions of the time did have "maladministration" as an impeachment ground. This does not mean that a given act may not be an instance *both* of "maladministration" *and* of "high crime" or "misdemeanor." It does mean that not *all* acts of "maladministration" are covered by the phrase actually accepted. This follows inevitably from Madison's ready acceptance of the phraseology now in the text; if "maladministration" was too "vague" for him, and "high Crimes and Misdemeanors" included all "maladministration," then he would surely have objected to the phrase actually accepted, as being even "vaguer" than the one rejected.

On the other hand, Mason's ready substitution of "high Crimes and Misdemeanors" indicates that *he* thought (and no voice was raised in doubt) that this new phrase would satisfactorily cover "many great and dangerous offenses" not reached by the words "treason" and "bribery"; its coverage was understood to be broad.

The whole colloquy just quoted seems to support the view that "high Crimes and Misdemeanors" ought to be conceived as offenses having about them some flavor of criminality. Mere "maladministration" was not to be enough for impeachment. This line may be a hard one to follow, but it is the line that the Framers quite clearly intended to draw, and we will have to try to follow it as best we can.

Several other things are to be noted about this colloquy of September 8, 1787. Madison's *reason* for objecting to "maladministration" as a ground was that the inclusion of this phrase would result in the president's holding his office "during pleasure of the Senate." In other words, if mere inefficient administration, or administration that did not accord with Congress's view of good policy, were enough for impeachment and removal, without any flavor of criminality or distinct wrongdoing, impeachment and removal would take on the character of a British parliamentary vote of "no confidence." The September 8 colloquy makes it very plain that this was not wanted, and certainly the phrase "high Crimes and Misdemeanors," whatever its vagueness at the edges, seems absolutely to forbid the removal of a president on the grounds that Congress does not on the whole think his administration of public affairs is good. This distinction may not be easy to draw in every case, but there are vast areas in which it is very clear. And it is perhaps the most important distinction of all, because it tells us—and Congress—that whatever may be the grounds for impeachment and removal, dislike of a president's policy is definitely not one of them, and ought to play *no* part in the decision on impeachment. There is every reason to think that most congressmen and senators are aware of this.

Before we leave this verbal exchange of a September 1787 day, one more little-noticed point must be mentioned. Mason says that we need more grounds for impeachment than treason and bribery alone *because we*

do not have the "bill of attainder," which he thinks to
have been a safeguard of the British Constitution. Let
us explore this.

The parliamentary bill of attainder, probably more
often than not directed at a public official, made past
conduct of the person attainted criminal, and imposed
punishment for it, without judicial trial and without any
necessary reference to prior law or to his offense's being
a crime under that prior law. The Framers of our Constitution looked on this procedure with such abhorrence that they prohibited its use not only by Congress
but even by the states. In the same clauses of the Constitution, they also prohibited, both as to Congress and
as to the states, the passage of any *"ex post facto* law"
—a law making past conduct criminal, with the result
that a person could be punished for doing something
which was not criminal when he did it. It will be seen
that these two monstrosities overlap in their coverage,
because the "bill of attainder," as said just above, may
impose penalties for any conduct, whether or not the
prior law dealt with that conduct at all.

Now Mason's assumption—which was not chal-
lenged and which seems clearly right—was that the
"bill of attainder" prohibition applied to any congressional actions dealing with the president. If this assumption is right, then it must also be true that the prohibition of *"ex post facto"* laws—laws making punishable
conduct that was not punishable when committed—is
equally applicable to Congress's dealings with the president. If this is right—and I would think it right whether
Mason had said what he did or not—then we have
established another boundary on "high Crimes and

Misdemeanors": that phrase must not be so interpreted as to make its operation in a given impeachment case equivalent to the operation of a bill of attainder, or of an *ex post facto* law, or of both.

When a congressman says, in effect, that Congress is entirely free to treat as impeachable any conduct it desires so to treat, he (or she) is giving a good textbook definition of a bill of attainder and an *ex post facto* law, rolled into one. Our Framers abhorred both these things, and we have never wavered from that abhorrence. It cannot be right for Congress to act toward the president as though these prohibitions did not exist. There may be no way to keep Congress from violating their letter or spirit, but the conscientious congressman has to feel them, in spirit at least, as bounding and confining the operation of the vague words, "high Crimes and Misdemeanors."

I say "in spirit," because the letter of these clauses cannot always apply. As pointed out above, in connection with the question of criminal character of the impeachment proceeding, the words "high Crimes and Misdemeanors" are themselves too vague to satisfy constitutional standards of reasonably clear warning, in criminal statutes as applied in the ordinary courts; in this technical sense, the application of the quoted phrase to concrete cases must often be *"ex post facto"* in practical effect. But the spirit and equity of the bill of attainder and *ex post facto* clauses can to a large extent be followed if we treat as impeachable those offenses, and only those, that a reasonable man might anticipate would be thought abusive and wrong, without reference to partisan politics or differences of opinion on policy. The approximation of this result necessitates exploration of some further issues.

The Relation between Impeachable Offenses and Ordinary Crimes

"Treason" and "bribery" are crimes, whether committed by the president or by anyone else. Is the meaning of the phrase "high Crimes and Misdemeanors" limited to ordinary crimes? Can a president lawfully be impeached and removed *only* for conduct which would also be punishable crime for anybody?

Some have contended for this interpretation. It would be easeful to be able to adopt it, because the vague phrase "high Crimes and Misdemeanors," would thus be lent all the precision of the statute book; agonized attempts properly to limit it, while at the same time leaving it properly ample scope, would be avoided. But I cannot think it remotely possible that this interpretation is right.

Suppose a president were to move to Saudi Arabia, so he could have four wives, and were to propose to conduct the office of the presidency by mail and wireless from there. This would not be a crime, provided his passport were in order. Is it possible that such gross and wanton neglect of duty could not be grounds for impeachment and removal?

Suppose a president were to announce that he would under no circumstances appoint any Roman Catholic to office and were rigorously to stick to this plan. I am not sure that this conduct would be punishable as crime, though it would clearly violate the constitutional provision that "no religious test" may ever be required for holding federal office. I cannot believe that it would make any difference whether this conduct was criminal for general purposes; it would clearly be a gross and anticonstitutional abuse of power, going to the life of our national unity, and it would be absurd to think that a president might not properly be removed for it.

Suppose a president were to announce and follow a policy of granting full pardons, in advance of indictment or trial, to all federal agents or police who killed anybody in line of duty, in the District of Columbia, whatever the circumstances and however unnecessary the killing. This would not be a crime, and probably could not be made a crime under the Constitution. But could anybody doubt that such conduct would be impeachable?

These extreme examples test the overall validity of the proposition that impeachable offenses must be ordinary indictable crimes as well, and I think the proposition fails the test. But the rather extravagant character of the illustrations makes another point: most *actual* presidential misdeeds, of a seriousness sufficient to warrant impeachment, are likely to be ordinary crimes as well. It is somewhat strange, indeed, that the question here being examined has assumed such prominence in our days, because most of the wrongful acts that have been seriously charged against an incumbent president are regular crimes—bribery, obstruction of justice, income-tax fraud, and so on— so that, as to these offenses, the issue under discussion here need not arise.

One important exception may be warlike activity. It

seems quite possible that military action, unauthorized by Congress and concealed from Congress, might at some point constitute such a murderous and insensate abuse of the commander-in-chief power as to amount to a "high Crime" or "Misdemeanor" for impeachment purposes, though not criminal in the ordinary sense. But (as I shall maintain later) precedents of the distant and recent past make it hard to establish knowing wrongfulness in most such cases. And the question, specifically, whether the long-secret 1973 Cambodian bombing could amount to an impeachable offense is complicated by the fact that, on its being revealed, Congress, by postponing until August 15, 1973, the deadline for its ending, would seem to have come close to ratifying it. One is sailing very close to the wind when one says, "You may do it till August 15, but it is an impeachable offense."

To resume the main line of thought here, I would conclude that the limitation of impeachable offenses to those offenses made generally criminal by statute is unwarranted—even absurd. But it remains true that the House of Representatives and the Senate must feel more comfortable when dealing with conduct clearly criminal in the ordinary sense, for as one gets further from that area it becomes progressively more difficult to be certain, as to any particular offense, that it is impeachable.

To turn the coin around, it would be comforting to our desire for certainty to be able to conclude, at least, that all regular crimes are impeachable offenses. But a moment's reflection would show that this, too, would produce absurdities. Suppose a president transported a

woman across a state line or even (so the Mann Act
reads) from one point to another within the District of
Columbia, for what is quaintly called an "immoral purpose." Or suppose a president did not immediately report to the nearest policeman that he had discovered
that one of his aides was a practicing homosexual—
thereby committing "misprision of a felony." Or suppose the president actively assisted a young White
House intern in concealing the latter's possession of
three ounces of marijuana—thus himself becoming
guilty of "obstruction of justice." Or suppose, to take a
real instance, that the presidential ladies' wearing of the
Saudi Arabian jewels technically constituted a criminal
"conversion" and that the president could be shown to
have been an "accomplice." Would it not be preposterous to think that any of this is what the Framers meant
when they referred to "Treason, Bribery, and other
high Crimes and Misdemeanors," or that any sensible
constitutional plan would make a president removable
on such grounds?

An Affirmative Approach to the Meaning of "high Crimes and Misdemeanors"

At this point, I think, we have to have recourse to
an old and quite sensible rule of legal construction.
This rule has, expectably, a Latin name, *"eiusdem
generis."* This phrase means "of the same kind," and
what the rule *eiusdem generis* says is that, when a general word occurs after a number of specific words, the
meaning of the general word ought often to be limited
to the *kind* or *class* of things within which the specific

words fall. Thus if I said, "Bring me some ice cream, or some candy, or something else good," I would think you had understood me well if you brought me a piece of good angel food cake, I would boggle a little, perhaps, if you brought me a good baked potato, and I would think you crazy or stupid or willful if you brought me a good book of sermons or a good bicycle tire pump.

Like all "rules" of interpretation, this one is not applicable everywhere. But it seems quite naturally to apply to the phrase "Treason, Bribery, or other high Crimes and Misdemeanors," and could help us toward identifying *both* those ordinary crimes which ought also to be looked upon as impeachable offenses, and those serious misdeeds, *not* ordinary crimes, which ought to be looked on as impeachable offenses, though not criminal in the ordinary sense.

The catch in applying this *eiusdem generis* rule is the difficulty (sometimes) of correctly pinning down the "kind" to which the specific items belong. In the present case, however, the "kind" to which "treason" and "bribery" belong is rather readily identifiable. They are offenses (1) which are extremely serious, (2) which in some way corrupt or subvert the political and governmental process, and (3) which are plainly wrong in themselves to a person of honor, or to a good citizen, regardless of words on the statute books.

Now this all may sound unbearably abstract, but this line of thought could solve many problems. Take the string of imagined cases used above to show the absurdity of limiting impeachable offenses to ordinary crimes —the examples of a president's migrating to Saudi

Arabia, or of his excluding Roman Catholics from appointment to office, or of his systematically pardoning all government police who kill anybody under any circumstances. Is it not the fact that these are serious assaults on the integrity of the processes of government, obviously wrong to any man of normal good sense, that makes us feel certain they must be impeachable offenses? On the other hand, take the common crimes that I gave as examples of criminal offenses which we would probably not think impeachable—transporting a woman for "immoral purposes," or easing things a bit for aides in trouble. If you agree with me that these offenses ought not to be held impeachable, is that not because they are not (as treason and bribery are) serious offenses against the nation or its governmental and political processes, obviously wrong, in themselves, to any person of honor?

Let us test the power of this kind of thought by applying it to a far from fanciful set of facts. Suppose a president were shown by convincing evidence to have used the federal tax system consistently and massively as a means of harassing and punishing his political opponents. As far as I know, this conduct is not criminal in the ordinary sense. But does such gross misuse of what is supposed to be a politically neutral arm of government not tend seriously to undermine and corrupt the political order? Is it not obviously wrong, to any man of ordinary honor? If these questions are answered "yes," then this offense, as lawyers might say, is *eiusdem generis,* of the same kind, with treason and bribery. It if *is* a crime under statute, then it is the kind of ordinary crime that ought to be held impeachable. If it is *not* a crime under statute, then it is the kind of offense which ought to be held impeachable, though not criminal in the ordinary sense. In both cases, this is because such an offense is, in the relevant ways, of the same kind as treason and bribery.

This rule will not work all the way; rules of interpretation rarely do. But the one obvious exception may be more apparent than real. Many common crimes—willful murder, for example—though not subversive of government or political order, might be so serious as to make a president simply unviable as a national leader; I cannot think that a president who had committed murder could not be removed by impeachment. But the underlying reason remains much the same; such crimes would so stain a president as to make his continuance in office dangerous to public order. Indeed, it may be this *prospective* tainting of the presidency that caused even treason and bribery to be made impeachable. So far as *punishment* goes, we could punish a traitorous or corrupt president after his term expired; we *remove* him principally because we fear he will do it again, or because a traitor or the taker of a bribe is not thinkable as a national leader.

Now this has been a long pull, but we have our hands on a good first approximation to a rational definition of an impeachable "high Crime or Misdemeanor." Omitting qualifications, and recognizing that the definition is only an approximation, I think we can say that "high Crimes and Misdemeanors," in the constitutional sense, ought to be held to be those offenses which are rather obviously wrong, whether or not "criminal," and which so seriously threaten the order of political society as to

make pestilent and dangerous the continuance in power
of their perpetrator. The fact that such an act is also
criminal helps, even if it is not essential, because a
general societal view of wrongness, and sometimes of
seriousness, is, in such a case, publicly and authoritatively recorded.

The phrase "high Crimes and Misdemeanors" carries
another connotation—that of *distinctness of offense.* It
seems that a charge of high crime or high misdemeanor
ought to be a charge of a definite act or acts, each of
which in itself satisfies the above requirements. General
lowness and shabbiness ought not to be enough. The
people take some chances when they elect a man to the
presidency, and I think this is one of them.

While on the topic of the relations between criminality and impeachability, let me remind the reader that
the president, like everybody else, is generally bound
by the criminal law. If something he has done is both
a crime and an impeachable offense, then, by express
constitutional provision, he may, after removal, be
tried again in the ordinary courts, and punished; this
provision was put in to avoid any possible plea of
"double jeopardy." If his criminal act is not held impeachable, it is still criminal. If the contention is up-
held (and I for one think it ought to be) that an
incumbent president cannot be put on trial in the
ordinary courts for ordinary crime, and if the crime he
is charged with is not an impeachable offense, the
simple and obvious solution would be either to indict
him and delay *trial* until after his term has expired,
or to delay *indictment* until after his term, with the
"Statute of Limitations," which bars prosecution after a

certain time, "tolled"—that is to say, stopped running —until the president's term is over. All these results could easily be attained by legitimate judicial techniques, but a simple Act of Congress could put the matter beyond doubt.

Application to Particular Problems

In what follows, I do not intend in any way to judge any real-life issue. Questions of exact fact and of evidence are always crucial, and it is not in any case my wish here to decide anything. But some questions are inevitably suggested by events, and can be dealt with tentatively.

Bribery

There is of course no problem about the impeachability of bribery; as indicated above, the problems in such cases are factual and are at their most difficult when motivation is concerned—the motivational connection between the thing of value received and the benefit conferred.

Income-Tax Fraud

Serious income-tax fraud by a president, particularly when the vehicle of such fraud is a set of papers resulting from his holding one government office, and when he might anticipate virtual immunity from serious audit because of his occupying the presidency, would seem definitely impeachable, in addition to being criminal. The offense seems akin to bribery, in that it uses office for corrupt gain; in any case, it undermines government, and confidence in government. A large-scale tax cheat is not a viable chief magistrate.

Use of Tax System to Harass Opponents

This has been discussed just above, as an illustration of the partial irrelevance of the ordinary criminal law to the finding of an impeachable offense. This offense not only thoroughly satisfies the canon of interpretation I have tried to elaborate, but also strikes close to the heart of what the Framers most feared in a president—*abuse of power*. Enforcement of any law, including the tax laws, must be to some extent discretionary. Perhaps the most dangerous (and certainly the most immoral) line of conduct an official can follow is that of using this discretion, which is given him for public purposes and is meant to be used neutrally, for the grossly improper purposes of menace and revenge. I should think that clearly evidenced and persistent misconduct of this kind is impeachable beyond a doubt.

Obviously, the same would be true of the harassing use of any governmental power meant to be neutrally employed; the tax system is only a conspicuous example.

Impoundment of Appropriated Funds for the Purpose of Destroying Authorized Programs

I, myself, feel no doubt that it is a violation of his constitutional duty for a president to use his discretionary power (which sometimes must be given him) over expenditures, for the improper purpose of dismantling altogether, or severely crippling, programs that have been regularly enacted in lawful form; this seems to me a violation of his duty to take care that the laws be *faithfully* executed. "Faithfully" is a word that does not keep company with the disingenuous pretense that economy is the motive, when the real motive is hostility to the law.

But that is only an opinion, and this is a gray area, wherein opinions may legitimately differ. The president operates under a statutory directive that total expenditure or debt not exceed a certain figure, and he may even have some residual responsibility not to see the country descend into financial ruin. He might think (though others would disagree) that these responsibilities were to be served best by cuts where his judgment advised they might least hurtfully be made, rather than by cuts across the board. Many appropriations, moreover, are phrased by Congress as *authorities* rather than as *duties* to spend. Finally, there seem to exist, in many cases, adequate judicial remedies for persons or governmental units who have a clear legal right to the "impounded" money, and a president might think that by "impounding" he is doing no more than referring a doubtful question to the courts.

On the whole, for all these reasons, I incline to think "impoundment" not an impeachable offense, though one ought never try to anticipate judgment on the flagrancy of some instance that might come to light. The problem is one that badly needs to be dealt with by Congress, using means short of impeachment—as to which, see Chapter 5.

Unauthorized Warlike Operations

This I find the most agonizing question of all. As a new matter, I should have thought that totally unauthorized entrance into hostilities, without any emergency or any immediate threat to the nation, was the grossest possible usurpation of power, clearly impeachable.

Unfortunately, it is not a new matter. The Bay of Pigs, for example, happened—and as far as I recall there was no talk of impeachment. There are many, many other precedents to which appeal can be made. Furthermore, there is often some fairly plausible claim of authorization in the particular case, and where experts disagree on justification, it is hard to find clear and wanton abuse of power. Moreover, it is the undoubted fact that the wrongness of unauthorized military action is likely to seem clear, on the whole, only to those who disapprove substantively of the particular intervention; would it be thought that an impeachable offense had been committed if our forces in the Mediterranean were ordered to intervene to keep the Syrians from taking Haifa?

Reluctantly, I have to conclude that only a very extreme and not now visible case ought to bring the impeachment weapon into play as a sanction against presidential warlike activity. Congress ought to deal with this matter comprehensively and clearly; if it did, then the president's violation of the congressional rules would be impeachable beyond a doubt, for the uncertainties generated by precedent would be cleared up. The so-called War Powers Resolution passed last year is so far from filling this need that the Administration, not without plausibility, could publicly toy with the idea that the resolution, supposedly a restraint on the president, actually authorized resumption of the Cambodian bombing that Congress had earlier ordered to be ended!

Improper Campaign Tactics

I know of no offense the impeachability of which more depends on the exact case shown by evidence. There must come a point at which the deliberate harassment of political opponents—the bugging of their offices, the circulation of known lies about them, the attributing to them of statements they never made, and so forth—takes on the character of deliberate and knowing wrong, as highly corruptive of the political process as is the actual bribery of voters. On the other hand, politics is known by all not to be croquet, and a certain amount of roughing up is expected. One could construct an endless series of hypothetical cases, and try to pronounce on each; the part of wisdom, in any such situation, is to suspend judgment until a real case is made out.

Here again, Congress could do much more than it has done to make clear what the rules are to be.

Obstruction of Justice

Here the question has to be whether the obstruction of justice has to do with public affairs and the political system; I would not think impeachable a president's act in helping a child or a friend of his to conceal misdeeds, unless the action were so gross as to make the

president unviable as a leader. In many cases his failure
to protect some people at some times might result in
his being held in contempt by the public. I would have
to say that the protection of their own people is in all
leaders, up to a point, a forgivable sin, and perhaps
even an expectable one; this consideration may go to
the issue of "substantiality," with which this chapter
closes. But the obstruction of justice is ordinarily a
wrong as well as a crime, and when it occurs in connection with governmental matters, and when its perpetrator is the person principally charged with taking care
that the laws be faithfully executed, there must come a
point at which excuses fail. Here again, the concrete-
ness of the evidentiary case is all important.

Some Final Considerations

The President's Responsibility
for Acts of his Subordinates

As to each possible impeachable offense, the question may arise of the president's responsibility for his
people's misdeeds.

Here I think we have to remember that it is the
president who must be found guilty of "high Crimes
and Misdemeanors." A simple attribution to him of
everything done by persons working under him is
totally incompatible with the flavor of criminality, of
moral wrong, in the quoted phrase. No chief of any
considerable enterprise could pass such a test.

At the other extreme, it goes without saying that
the president (like anybody else) is totally responsible
for what he commands, suggests, or ratifies.

The difficult area is in between, the area of "negligence." I would find it impossible to qualify simple carelessness in supervision as a "high Crime or Misdemeanor"; perfect freedom from negligence is for the angels. At this point, however, the general law furnishes us with a valuable concept. When carelessness is so gross and habitual as to be evidence of *indifference* to wrongdoing, it may be in effect equivalent to ratification of wrongdoing. If I drive my car in an utterly reckless manner, and someone is injured, the case is not merely that I have been guilty of "negligence," but that I have so behaved as to show indifference to whether somebody got hurt or not. Gross and habitual indifference of this kind is more than mere negligence, and might well be held to amount to impeachable conduct.

Here, as in so many cases, everything depends on what the evidence in a case actually shows, but these are the right lines along which to sort out the evidence.

Good-Faith Belief in the Rightness of an Act

This concept has figured in this book at several points, in the discussion of particular offenses. Belief in the lawfulness or rightness of an action, in order to be a defense, must be such belief as a reasonable person could hold. A reasonable man could think selective impoundment of funds both lawful and right, but no reasonable man could think it right to use the tax system for partisan political purposes.

Here, again, Congress has an enormous role to play. A cleancut declaration, by Congress, that a given line of conduct is wrong, makes it much more difficult for a reasonable man to claim reliance on his own assessment of the matter. Congress has the power, within wide limits, to make presidential conduct criminal; where this was done, no subsequent president could be heard to say that he was not fully warned.

Substantiality

"Not all presidential misconduct is sufficient to constitute grounds for impeachment. There is a further requirement—substantiality." These words occur in the Conclusion to the House Judiciary Committee's Staff Report on Constitutional Grounds for Presidential Impeachment (the full citation is in Appendix A).

Undoubtedly this is true, but the concept is an extremely difficult one to handle. Does it mean "substantiality of the single offense" or "substantiality of all offenses proved, taken together"? Either alternative is dangerous. Should a president be impeached and removed when he has committed no single offense which would in itself justify removal? Would not an affirmative answer encourage the "stacking" of rather petty charges? On the other hand, would a president who has committed a number of offenses, offenses that, one by one, satisfy every criterion for impeachability except substantiality, not at some point have shown himself unfit for office?

To me, the first of these dangers is by far the greater, for it merges with fatal ease into the peril of an overall judgment of mere unfitness—quite outside the plain meaning of "high Crimes and Misdemeanors." The question will present itself in any particular case in highly concrete form. The answer, when answer must be given, must probably be to some extent political; law can lead us to the point where "substantiality" becomes the issue, but law cannot tell us what is "substantial" for the purpose of decision. We may justifiably hope that those who have to make this political judgment will see it as high-political, and not as having any connection with partisan politics, or with views on policy.

A Note on History

The phrase "high Crimes and Misdemeanors" comes to us out of English law and practice, starting (as far as we know) in 1386. It frequently figured in impeachment of officers. The English history seems to establish with some clarity that the English did not understand the phrase as denoting *only* common crimes, but in some sense saw it as including serious misconduct in office, whether or not punishable as crime in the ordinary courts. Beyond that, I have to confess that I can read no clear message. Sometimes the English cases seem to prove too much, treating as "high Crimes and Misdemeanors" petty acts of maladministration which no sensible person could think impeachable offenses in a president, or in anybody. This leaves us right where we were, so far as line-drawing is concerned. In many cases, "impeachment," a charge brought by the House of Commons, was not followed by conviction in the House of Lords, the finally responsible body; this makes the precedent a truncated one at best. Further, although many of the Framers of our Constitution undoubtedly knew in at least a general way of the English usage, and certainly borrowed the term "high Crimes and Misdemeanors" from that usage, it is hard for me to think that many of them, or many people at the state ratifying conventions, or many members of the late eighteenth-century American public, could have carried about, ever-present in their minds, much of the superabundant learning which in modern times has been developed on the subject. Nor does that learning, interesting as it is intrinsically, seem to me to eventuate in the unequivocal validation of any very precise view of the exact boundaries of the phrase's meaning.

If this history were to be canvassed here, this would be a very different (and much fatter) book—and I would be a very different (and probably much leaner) person. I have to say, on my own responsibility, that the English historical material I have seen does not seem to stand in the way of our working out, in any great case in our own times, a sensible concept of the meaning of "high Crimes and Misdemeanors," suitable to the spirit and structure of our Constitution.

All the American precedents are handily collected in the above-mentioned report by the staff of the Committee on the Judiciary of the House of Representatives, 93rd Congress, 2nd Session, *Constitutional Grounds for Presidential Impeachment.* But these precedents, too, fall far short of furnishing a well-rounded and well-supported answer to the question of the meaning of "high Crimes and Misdemeanors." There have been thirteen impeachments in all. Ten of them were of federal judges; four of these were acquitted, four were convicted, and two resigned, with the result that no Senate verdict was given. One senator was impeached; the Senate voted that it had no jurisdiction to convict a senator on impeachment, so that the case was dismissed without verdict. One secretary of war was impeached; he was acquitted on all Articles, but the force of the acquittal is clouded by the fact that an indeterminate number of senators may (or may not) have voted to acquit dominantly or wholly on the ground that the man had already resigned. The remaining case was that of President Andrew Johnson. He was impeached, substantially, for having removed the secretary of war, a holdover from Lincoln's administration, in alleged violation of a Tenure of Office Act passed by the Reconstruction Congress, and for attempting to bring disgrace and ridicule on Congress —itself a ridiculous charge. He was acquitted, but by a vote just one short of the two-thirds needful to convict; such an "acquittal" is not a satisfactory legal precedent on "impeachable offense."

Now it is very plain that these American precedents speak with little clarity to new issues. Like the English precedents, they pretty clearly show a pattern of going beyond ordinary crimes for impeachable offenses: intoxication on the bench, for example, figures in several of the judicial impeachments. On the other hand, an acquittal blunts any precedent.

In the one presidential case, that of Johnson, the acquittal was almost certainly not on the facts, but on the belief that no impeachable offense had been charged—but with the weakness as precedent just mentioned. Moreover, the Johnson impeachment is, to say the least, by no means universally regarded today as a paradigm of propriety or of unimpassioned law.

On the whole, again, what this history really says is that no historical impediment exists to a sensible, reasoned treatment, right now, of the problem of the meaning of "high Crimes and Misdemeanors." The history of impeachment, like the history of most serious subjects, may conduce to underlying wisdom, but decision is for us, today.

4. Impeachment and the Courts

Is There to be Judicial Review of the Senate's Verdict on Impeachment?

The process of presidential impeachment, and trial thereon, culminates in a judgment of the Senate, either that the president is not guilty, or that he is guilty on one or more of the Articles of Impeachment voted by the House, and is to be removed from office (perhaps with the additional penalty of disqualification to hold office in the future). Is this judgment of conviction final, or is it in some manner appealable, to the Supreme Court or elsewhere?

Now before we take this question apart technically, let us just sit back a moment and consider the straight sense of it. The most powerful maxim of constitutional law is that its rules ought to make sense. Let us try to imagine the situation which could be produced by providing judicial review of a senatorial judgment of removal.

Picture, if you will, a president whose conduct has attracted such unfavorable notice as to be thoroughly investigated by the Judiciary Committee of the House of Representatives. The result of this investigation has been a formal recommendation to the whole House that Articles of Impeachment be voted. After the

fullest debate, with the attention of the country fo-
cused on the issue, the House concludes that the president ought indeed to be impeached of "Treason,
Bribery, or other high Crimes and Misdemeanors." All
questions of law and fact have now been thoroughly
canvassed in one House, with a result adverse to the
president. Next, the Articles of Impeachment go to
the Senate, which is put upon special solemn oath, and
which sits in judgment with the chief justice of the
Supreme Court presiding. The Senate, after plenary
trial and fullest argument of counsel, and after debate
among senators on fact and law, votes by a two-thirds
majority to convict and remove the president.

The president now appeals to the Supreme Court.
The jurisdiction of that Court over the appeal is to say
the least quite unclear, but it takes jurisdiction anyway.
On the merits, the Court disagrees with the House and
with the Senate on some point, let us say, as to the
meaning of "high Crimes and Misdemeanors," or on
some procedural question of weight (perhaps dividing
5 to 4, perhaps filing nine opinions no five of which
espouse the same reasoning). *So it puts the impeached
and convicted president back in for the rest of his term.*
And we all live happily ever after.

I don't think I possess the resources of rhetoric adequate to characterizing the absurdity of that position.
With what aura of legitimacy would a thus-reinstated
chief magistrate be surrounded? Who would salute?
When a respectably dressed Londoner approached the
Duke of Wellington, saying "Mr. Smith, I believe,"
the Duke replied, "If you believe that, you'll believe
anything." I would say the same of anyone who can

believe that there is hidden away somewhere, in the interstitial silences of a Constitution formed by men of practical wisdom, a command that could bring about such a preposterous result as the judicial reinstatement of a president solemnly convicted, pursuant to the constitutional forms, of "Treason, Bribery, or other high Crimes and Misdemeanors." (I may say, parenthetically, that if you are one who believes that sound constitutional law cannot make nonsense, or generate absurdities, you can rest on that correct belief and skip the rest of this chapter.)

If such a result seemed to be commanded by explicit language in the Constitution, then I should think the Supreme Court would try desperately to find some loophole through which to escape exercising this absurd function. But the Constitution contains no such command. The command has to be worked out, if at all, on the basis of elaborate inference piled on inference.

The standard justifications of judicial review do not support it. Courts decide constitutional questions when these arise in cases over which they have jurisdiction. The Supreme Court, as a quick perusal of Article III will show, does not have "original" jurisdiction over any kind of suit seeking to overturn a senatorial judgment removing the president. The question of its "appellate" jurisdiction (the jurisdiction to hear and decide appeals) is more complicated. On the face of Article III, the Supreme Court has "appellate" jurisdiction over all the cases brought within the judicial power by that Article. One of these categories is "all Cases, in Law and Equity, arising under this Consti-

tution. . . ." If the Supreme Court's appellate power
over impeachment judgments is located anywhere, it is
here.

Many objections to its being found here come
readily to mind. The terms "Law" and "Equity" were
and are thoroughly established terms of art, referring
to the two sorts of regular judicial courts existing, in
England and here, at the time of the adoption of the
Constitution; impeachments are, in this well-known
technical sense, neither in "Law" nor in "Equity." This
reading chimes exactly with the whole tenor of Article
III, which has to do with regular judicial business in
ordinary courts, except for a passage making it clear
that jury trial was to play no part in impeachment.
This latter provision, as a study of successive drafts of
the Constitution will show, was left in the judiciary
Article (now Article III) when impeachment trial was
shifted from the Supreme Court to the Senate, and
therefore to the Article (now Article I) dealing with
the legislative branch. (The chief importance of this
shift is discussed below.) It was doubtless left in place
because its main thrust—a general rule of trial by jury
—belonged in the judiciary article, and the reservation
on impeachments had to be left in it, lest there be mis-
understanding. The occurrence of the word "impeachment" in the judiciary Article (III) has therefore no
tendency to establish that impeachment is in any way
an Article III matter. Indeed, close algebraic reasoning would lead to the conclusion that impeachment,
and trial thereon, are not within the Article III "judicial power" at all, for that "judicial power" is a power
that Congress may "vest," in the first instance, in in-

ferior courts of its own creation (except as to cases, of which impeachment is not one, which are within the Supreme Court's "original" jurisdiction), and it cannot do that as to impeachment proceedings.

There is no inconsistency here with the position I have taken, above, that the trial in the Senate is to be looked on as *similar* to a "judicial" trial, and that senators should perceive their role in these terms. A trial that is "judicial" in the sense that it aims at fairness, impartiality, and decision according to law, need not, for that reason, fall within the Article III "judicial power," which concerns, up, down, and sideways, the jurisdiction of ordinary courts of justice.

Further support here is found in the fact that, when the Constitutional Convention moved the trial of impeachments from the Supreme Court to the Senate (as to which removal see below) it dropped "impeachment" altogether from the list which later became, by stylistic revision, the list defining the Article III "judicial power."

But these algebraic reasonings, which are really alien to the spirit of constitutional law, need not be mathematically conclusive; they need show no more than that there is an escape, thank Heaven, from the preposterous situation that we would face if the Constitution unmistakeably commanded judicial review of convictions on impeachment.

There are other, lower roads of escape. As it came from the hands of its draftsmen, the present Article III of the Constitution might appear affirmatively to grant appellate jurisdiction (jurisdiction to hear appeals) to the Supreme Court:

In all the other Cases before mentioned [i.e., those within the federal "judicial power"], the supreme Court *shall have* appellate Jurisdiction, both as to Law and Fact, *with such Exceptions,* and under such Regulations as the Congress shall make. (Emphasis added)

But the entire history of the Supreme Court's appellate jurisdiction, as shaped by Congress's exercise of its own "exceptions" power, unequivocally disaffirms this interpretation. It has been held with invariant uniformity, since the beginning, that the comprehensive and detailed Acts of Congress *granting* appellate jurisdiction to the Supreme Court, in carefully named classes of cases (Acts which are now part of a painstakingly considered codification), by implication *except* from that jurisdiction all cases *not* named, and that these jurisdictional Acts thus exercise, as to all cases not named by them, the congressional power to make *"exceptions"* to the Supreme Court's appellate jurisdiction—a power expressly given to Congress in the part of Article III just quoted. Thus, in practical effect, the Supreme Court does *not* exercise appellate jurisdiction unless Congress grants that jurisdiction in a statute; every single appeal ever filed in the Supreme Court begins with a paper wherein it is indispensable that the *congressional statute* giving jurisdiction be cited. Of course Congress has never included, in any such statute, a grant to the Supreme Court of appellate power over senatorial judgments in impeachment cases. It is quite reasonable, then (even if one believes, as I never could, that impeachment verdicts fell within the Article III appellate judicial power before Congress acted), to hold that Congress has "excepted" it, so that it cannot be exercised.

Even if both these arguments fail to convince, at least the "exceptions" power remains, and Congress might at any time exercise it to *remove* impeachment matters from the appellate jurisdiction of the Supreme Court. The one Supreme Court precedent on this subject held that Congress could effectively abolish the Court's jurisdiction over an appeal *even after it was filed and argued.* The very fact that Congress could do this strengthens the position that the judicial appellate power never extended to impeachment verdicts, for it would be a virtual nullity, hardly worth the labor of constructing, when Congress could knock it down at will.

All these arguments are strongly buttressed by the fact that the 1787 Constitutional Convention, after debate and over prestigeful opposition, moved impeachment trials out of the Supreme Court and into the Senate. This was done, as one would expect, for the quite straightforward reason that the Convention thought the Senate, rather than the Supreme Court, should deal with impeachments. Why else?

So far as I can find, not one syllable pronounced or written in or around the time of the adoption of the Constitution gives the faintest color to the supposition that the Supreme Court was expected to have anything to do with impeachments, or the trial thereof, or appeals thereon.

What about the lower courts? Suppose a convicted and removed president were to bring a civil action in the Federal District Court for the District of Columbia seeking a judicial declaration that he had been wrongfully convicted, and asking for a mandatory injunction (perhaps against Congress and the White House Guards as parties defendant) commanding his reinstallation in office.

Now the lower courts are *created* by Congress, under Article III, and their jurisdiction is wholly controlled by Congress. The District Courts (and I apologize for being so solemn about this matter, but if I can I want to lay it to rest once and for all) have jurisdiction (*conferred upon them by Congress* in pursuance of Article III) over civil actions, wherein the amount in controversy is over $10,000, "arising under the Constitution and laws of the United States." Is the convicted (and assumedly ex-) president's suit one of that description? Cases "arising under" maritime law, although that law is now firmly considered a part of *national* law, made so by the Constitution, have been held not to be suits "arising under" the Constitution or laws of the United States, on the quite sensible ground that, regardless of the breadth of the statutory language considered abstractly, the history of the subject makes it most unlikely that Congress ever intended to include maritime cases within this general language. Is it possible to say any less than that of the claim of a removed president to be reinstated, or even to get his salary? Is it so much as conceivable that Congress, in putting this general language ("all civil actions arising under the Constitution . . .") on the statute book, intended to give the lower federal courts jurisdiction to annul and undo impeachment verdicts? (Here, again,

Congress might easily at any time take away the jurisdictional grant, if there were any realism in the fear
that a court would try to trap Congress in this way.)

There is, so far as I can find, not a shred of affirmative historical evidence that the Framers and ratifiers
of the Constitution ever thought for one moment that
the *lower* courts were to deal with impeachment questions. It is quite incredible, given the great amount of
attention paid to impeachment procedure, that this
possibility never would have been mentioned, if in fact
it had been thought a serious possibility.

Now as a practical matter no court is ever going to
succeed in putting an impeached and convicted president back in office; it is most unlikely that any court
will try. The only thing that could result from a judicial
attempt to do this would be a terrible constitutional
crisis. For the ultimate latent weakness of judicial
power (kept latent only by the courts' respect for the
law that creates them) is that the duty to obey a judicial
decree exists only when the court that utters the decree
is acting within its jurisdiction. This rule is sensibly
softened by some concession to courts of the right to
determine their own jurisdiction. But a court acting in
wide excess of its jurisdiction has no claim to being
obeyed. If the Supreme Court, or any other federal
court, were to order reinstatement of an impeached and
convicted president, there would be, to say the least,
a very grave and quite legitimate doubt whether that
decree had any title to being obeyed, or whether it was,
on the other hand, a decree as widely outside judicial
jurisdiction as would be a judicial order to Congress to
increase the penalty for counterfeiting. To cite the most

frightening consequence, our military commanders
would have to decide for themselves which president
they were bound to obey, the reinstated one or his successor. I think I would advise them that they must obey
the successor; others would undoubtedly give the contrary advice. Is it possible that our Constitution set up
such a situation as that?

I have thought it worthwhile to argue this point fully
because, while I cannot conceive that any court would
so have lost the faculty of judgment as to try to undo a
Senate sentence of removal on impeachment, I think
it well that, so far as possible, the fundamental uncon-
stitutionality of such action be publicly accepted, precisely because, as I have briefly pointed out above, the
wide diffusion of this concept—that the courts have no
role to fill—makes very plain to all the *final* responsibility of the Senate, on facts and on law. It would be
most unfortunate if the notion got about that the Senate's verdict were somehow tentative. The crucial
senatorial vote should be taken, and should be known
to be taken, with full knowledge that there is no appeal. No senator should be encouraged to think he can
shift to any court responsibility for an unpalatable or
unpopular decision.

The dissemination of the "judicial review" idea
could be most unfortunate in another way; if a removed president tried it, and had his case (as would
almost surely happen) dismissed for want of jurisdiction, he might be able, though quite wrongly, to per-
suade a part of the people that he had been denied his
rightful day in court.

I would conclude, then, with a paraphrase of the

well-known saying of the country banker, when he was asked about cashing a check for a stranger. He said, "There are ten rules about cashing checks for strangers. The first rule is, 'Never cash a check for a stranger.' The other nine rules don't matter." There are ten rules about judicial review of the judgments of the Senate on impeachments. The first rule is that the courts have, in this, no part at all to play. The other nine rules don't matter.

May Congress Use the Federal Courts to Assist in Impeachment Investigations?

This question stands on a very different footing. It might very well happen, for example, that the House of Representatives Judiciary Committee, or some other committee charged with investigation that might lead to impeachment, would need the aid of judicial process to procure testimony or documents. For example, a recalcitrant witness might be jailed by court order, on application of the committee, until he agreed to testify. The practical and jurisdictional complexities here are many, but these complexities need not be explored here. The point is that no general *constitutional* objection prevents Congress from enlisting the aid of the courts in ways ancillary to its own responsibilities.

Some problems, however, are salient and pervasive. Once any matter (such as, to pursue the example just given, the use of the judicial civil contempt power to compel testimony) is brought into court, the one thing Congress cannot do is to tell the court how it must decide the case. A court, for example, might conclude that the witness was privileged *not* to testify, and free him. To this extent, Congress (very properly) loses control of its own business when it brings that business into court.

Secondly, judicial proceedings are *timed* largely as the judges see fit; in consequence, bringing business into court means surrendering one's own timing plan.

These considerations probably will prevent any very frequent recourse by either House of Congress to the courts, for aid in impeachment proceedings. Each House has a considerable inherent power to punish for contempt, without recourse to the courts.

5. Short of Impeachment

In some tribal cultures, the system of legal sanctions is very simple. There are two possible ways of dealing with deviants: toleration and death. A persistent troublemaker is endured for a long time, perhaps not without grumbling, but without any effective attempt at control. Then he commits some action which is just one thing too many—the last straw. After some informal consultation, he is speared, or shoved out into the cold to freeze. There is only one sanction—the sanction of elimination. No finer-graded system of control is conceived.

Sometimes we seem to be talking as though a system something like that were all we have for dealing with a president or with the presidency. A great many people are dissatisfied with what the presidency has become and is becoming. We feel things have gone too far. So we start consulting among ourselves, and at last reach for the spear of impeachment.

Of course it can be true that things may have gone too far in any given case. Elimination may in a rare case be the only way. But we have, let us hope, a long future to face together, we and our presidents. It might be well to consider whether a more finely graded system of controls might be developed.

Events have shown that the presidency, however

much its incumbent may aspire to and scheme for strength, is actually quite weak, without means of defense against a resolute Congress. The spectacle has perhaps not edified. But it has demonstrated, to a pathological degree, something which is a good thing in smaller amounts: the presidency has little firm constitutional power of its own. A skimming of the Constitution confirms this all the way. The president's power to appoint officers is in the hands of the Senate. The commander-in-chief power is subject to such control as inheres in Congress's powers to declare war, to raise and support the armed forces, and to enact regulations for their governance. The "foreign relations" power is deeply bitten into by Congress's power over foreign commerce, while power over the internal economy could be made plenary through exercise of Congress's power over commerce among the states, and of its power to tax and spend "for the general welfare." And underlying everything is the congressional power to appropriate (or to refuse to appropriate) the money that makes the political world go 'round.

In brief, Congress is by no means in the position of having to sit idly by, counting up grievances, until time comes to call a council of elders and sharpen the impeachment spear. Congress (as is perfectly plain on the face of the Constitution) can exercise just about any control it wants on the operations of government, including, in vast measure if not entirely, the actions of the president.

Correspondingly, Congress must share the responsibility for the twentieth-century aggrandizement of the presidency. Much of congressional complaint about that aggrandizement is shadowboxing, or at best a wail for the vanished horse, emanating from a man who habitually and chronically just would not lock the stable door.

Take the matter of war. The Viet Nam war went on a long time. There was continual complaint in Congress. Why didn't Congress refuse to appropriate money for prosecuting the war? That refusal couldn't even have been vetoed, because it would not have been a congressional action, but a congressional inaction. Why didn't Congress pass a concurrent resolution (which, being a mere statement of congressional opinion, is not subject to veto) declaring in unmistakeable terms the view that the war was immoral and against the country's interest? Would not such a resolution, though without legal force, have destroyed the moral basis of the war, to an extent making virtually necessary its speedy liquidation? Maybe not, but would there have been any harm in trying?

Consider the matter of "impoundment"—the refusal by the president to spend appropriated money on programs not to his liking. Many of the statutes in question are quite unclear as to whether the expenditure is bindingly directed or merely authorized. Congress has not yet passed a general law clarifying the limits on the president's power to "impound," though such a statute, unquestionably constitutional, would greatly clarify the guidelines confining a presidential power which is to some extent necessary.

Why should Congress not pass a law, with severe penalties for all concerned, stringently forbidding the use of the income-tax system to harass political enemies

—or its use for any purpose other than revenue-raising, with the rain of audit falling at random on friends and "enemies" alike?

There has been much concern about the use of public funds for what are essentially personal purposes, such as the upkeep and repair of the president's houses. This matter is plainly amenable to legislative control; no president would dare veto an Act setting bounds on this, and if he did, and if passage over his veto failed, it would still be possible for Congress to refuse further appropriations for these purposes.

One could go on like this all day. Congress is top dog—if (and what an enormous if) it wants to be.

Let us take the more complex matter of *information*. A great deal of Congress's weakness comes from its not having developed a system for procuring a continual flow to itself of information of all kinds from the departments and agencies. This has little to do with presidential "confidentiality"; I am not talking now about the president's own conversations in the Oval Office, but about data on wheat production in the Department of Agriculture. Almost none of such information is even arguably "privileged" against congressional access and use. The task is for Congress to create the conduits and reservoirs to bring in and hold ready this information. Knowledge is power, above all in politics; Congress cannot be innovative and creative unless it insists on having fluid access to the knowledge now stored in the agencies and departments.

Or take the possible use of the concurrent resolution, not subject to veto, as a means of expressing formally both the convictions and the intentions of

Congress. I have already mentioned how such a resolution, though without force as law, might have destroyed the moral basis for the Viet Nam war. Might it not in other cases be used to censure, or to register some more mildly worded disapproval of, actions of the president? Is it conceivable that such censure, by a Congress to which the president must look for support, would have no effect?

In the long haul, we must put the spear of impeachment back in the closet, though coated with cosmoline against rust. There are infinitely numerous milder ways in which the elephantiasis of the presidency can be treated.

We need, too, to rehabilitate the presidency. It is an office that on the whole has served us well. It is in bad shape.

But that is another story. The most critical point possible in the relations of Congress and the presidency is that of the actual imminence of impeachment proceedings. If this book has a single thought underlying all its particularities, it is that, when this most critical of points is reached, it is utterly vital to the health of our polity that the needful proceedings, whatever their event, be handled lawfully. Perhaps the most important thing the citizen can strive for, in this context, is an appreciation of the constraints which this need for visible and faultless lawfulness puts upon those bodies —the House and the Senate—who are charged with responsibility. On the foundation of that lawfulness, and on it only, a better future may be built.

Appendix A: Bibliography*

The Association of the Bar of the City of New York, *The Law of Presidential Impeachment and Removal* (1974). The study concludes that impeachment is not limited to criminal offenses but extends to conduct undermining governmental integrity.

Bayard, James, *A Brief Exposition of the Constitution of the United States,* (Hogan & Thompson, Philadelphia, 1833). A treatise on American constitutional law concluding that ordinary legal forms ought not to govern the impeachment process.

Berger, Raoul, *Impeachment: The Constitutional Problems,* (Harvard University Press, Cambridge, 1973). A critical historical survey of English and American precedents concluding that criminality is not a requirement for impeachment.

Bestor, Arthur, "Book Review, Berger, *Impeachment: The Constitutional Problems,*" 49 *Wash. L. Rev.* 225 (1973). A review concluding that the thrust of impeachment in English history and as viewed by the framers was to reach political conduct injurious to the commonwealth, whether or not the conduct was criminal.

Boutwell, George, *The Constitution of the United States at the End of the First Century,* (D. C. Heath & Co., Boston,

---

*This bibliography is from the House Judiciary Committee Staff Report on Constitutional Grounds for Presidential Impeachment, 93d Congress, 2d Session. The comments are those of the compilers of the report.

1895). A discussion of the Constitution's meaning after a century's use, concluding that impeachment had not been confined to criminal offenses.

Brant, Irving, *Impeachment: Trials & Errors,* (Alfred Knopf, New York, 1972). A descriptive history of American impeachment proceedings, which concludes that the Constitution should be read to limit impeachment to criminal offenses, including the common law offense of misconduct in office and including violations of oaths of office.

Bryce, James, *The American Commonwealth,* (Macmillan Co., New York, 1931) (reprint). An exposition on American government concluding that there was no final decision as to whether impeachment was confined to indictable crimes. The author notes that in English impeachments there was no requirement for an indictable crime.

Burdick, Charles, *The Law of the American Constitution,* (G. T. Putnam & Sons, New York, 1922). A text on constitutional interpretation concluding that misconduct in office by itself is grounds for impeachment.

Dwight, Theodore, "Trial by Impeachment," 6 *Am. L. Reg.* (*N.S.*) 257 (1867). An article on the eve of President Andrew Johnson's impeachment concluding that an indictable crime was necessary to make out an impeachable offense.

Etridge, George, "The Law of Impeachment" 8 *Miss. L. J.* 283 (1936). An article arguing that impeachable offenses had a definite meaning discoverable in history, statute and common law.

Feerick, John, "Impeaching Federal Judges: A Study of the Constitutional Provisions," 39 *Fordham L. Rev.* 1 (1970). An article concluding that impeachment was not limited to indictable crimes but extended to serious misconduct in office.

Fenton, Paul, "The Scope of the Impeachment Power," 65

Nw. U. L. Rev. 719 (1970). A law review article concluding that impeachable offenses are not limited to crimes, indictable or otherwise.

Finley, John and John Sanderson, *The American Executive and Executive Methods,* (Century Co., New York, 1908). A book on the presidency concluding that impeachment reaches misconduct in office, which was a common law crime embracing all improprieties showing unfitness to hold office.

Foster, Roger, *Commentaries on the Constitution of the United States,* (Boston Book Co., Boston, 1896), vol. I. A discussion of constitutional law concluding that in light of English and American history any conduct showing unfitness for office is an impeachable offense.

Lawrence, William, "A Brief of the Authorities upon the Law of Impeachable Crimes and Misdemeanors," *Congressional Globe Supplement,* 40th Congress, 2d Session, at 41 (1868). An article at the time of Andrew Johnson's impeachment concluding that indictable crimes were not needed to make out an impeachable offense.

Note, "The Exclusiveness of the Impeachment Power under The Constitution," 51 *Harv. L. Rev.* 330 (1937). An article concluding that the Constitution included more than indictable crimes in its definition of impeachable offenses.

Note, "Vagueness in the Constitution: The Impeachment Power," 25 *Stan. L. Rev.* 908 (1973). This book review of the Berger and Brant books concludes that neither author satisfactorily answers the question whether impeachable offenses are limited to indictable crimes.

Pomeroy, John, *An Introduction to the Constitutional Law of the United States,* (Hurd and Houghton, New York 1870). A consideration of constitutional history which concludes that impeachment reached more than ordinary indictable offenses.

Rawle, William, *A View of the Constitution of the United States,* (P. H. Nicklin, Philadelphia, 1829, 2 vol. ed.). A discussion of the legal and political principles underlying the Constitution, concluding on this issue that an impeachable offense need not be a statutory crime, but that reference should be made to nonstatutory law.

Rottschaefer, Henry, *Handbook of American Constitutional Law,* (West, St. Paul, 1939). A treatise on the Constitution concluding that impeachment reached any conduct showing unfitness for office, whether or not a criminal offense.

Schwartz, Bernard, *A Commentary on the Constitution of the United States,* vol I, (Macmillan, New York, 1963). A treatise on various aspects of the Constitution which concludes that there was no settled definition of the phrase "high Crimes and Misdemeanors," but that it did not extend to acts merely unpopular with Congress. The author suggests that criminal offenses may not be the whole content of the Constitution on this point, but that such offenses should be a guide.

Sheppard, Furman, *The Constitutional Textbook,* (George W. Childs, Philadelphia, 1855). A text on Constitutional meaning concluding that impeachment was designed to reach any serious violation of public trust, whether or not a strictly legal offense.

Simpson, Alex., *A Treatise on Federal Impeachments,* (Philadelphia Bar Association, Phila., 1916) (reproduced in substantial part in 64 *U. Pa. L.*) *Rev.* 651 (1916). After reviewing English and American impeachments and available commentary, the author concludes that an indictable crime is not necessary to impeach.

Story, Joseph, *Commentaries on the Constitution of the United States,* vol. 1, 5th edition, (Little, Brown & Co., Boston, 1891). A commentary by an early Supreme Court Justice who concludes that impeachment reached conduct not indictable under the criminal law.

Thomas, David, "The Law of Impeachment in the United States," 2 *Am. Pol. Sci. Rev.* 378 (1908). A political scientist's view on impeachment concluding that the phrase "high Crimes and Misdemeanors" was meant to include more than indictable crimes. The author argues that English parliamentary history, American precedent, and common law support his conclusion.

Tucker, John, *The Constitution of the United States,* (Callaghan & Co., Chicago, 1899), vol. 1. A treatise on the Constitution concluding that impeachable offenses embrace willful violations of public duty whether or not a breach of positive law.

Wasson, Richard, *The Constitution of the United States: Its History and Meaning,* (Bobbs-Merrill, Indianapolis, 1927). A short discussion of the Constitution concluding that criminal offenses do not exhaust the reach of the impeachment power of Congress. Any gross misconduct in office was thought an impeachable offense by this author.

Watson, David, *The Constitution of the United States,* (Callaghan & Co., Chicago, 1910), volumes I and II. A treatise on Constitutional interpretation concluding that impeachment reaches misconduct in office whether or not criminal.

Wharton, Francis, *Commentaries on Law,* (Kay & Bro., Philadelphia, 1884). A treatise by an author familiar with both criminal and Constitutional law. He concludes that impeachment reached willful misconduct in office that was normally indictable at common law.

Willoughby, Westel, *The Constitutional Law of the United States,* vol. III, 2nd edition, (Baker, Voorhis & Co., New York, 1929). The author concludes that impeachment was not limited to offenses made criminal by federal statute.

Yankwich, Leon, "Impeachment of Civil Officers under the Federal Constitution," 26 *Geo. L. Rev.* 849 (1938). A law review article concluding that impeachment covers general official misconduct whether or not a violation of law.

Appendix B

The following are the provisions in the Constitution most relevant to the subject of this book, with emphasis added:

ARTICLE I

. . . .

Section 2. . . . .

[5] The House of Representatives shall chuse their Speaker and other Officers; *and shall have the sole Power of Impeachment.*

Section 3. . . . .

[6] The Senate shall have the sole Power to try all Impeachments. When sitting for that Purpose, they shall be on Oath or Affirmation. When the President of the United States is tried, the Chief Justice shall preside: And no Person shall be convicted without the Concurrence of two thirds of the Members present.

[7] Judgment in Cases of Impeachment shall not extend further than to removal from Office, and disqualification to hold and enjoy any Office of honor, Trust, or Profit under the United States: but the Party convicted shall nevertheless be liable and subject to Indictment, Trial, Judgment, and Punishment, according to Law.

. . . .

Section 9. . . . .

[3] No Bill of Attainder or ex post facto Law shall be passed.

. . . .

Section 10. [1] No State shall enter into any Treaty, Alliance, or Confederation; grant Letters of Marque and Reprisal; coin Money; emit Bills of Credit; make any Thing but gold and silver Coin a Tender in Payment of Debts; *pass any Bill of Attainder, ex post facto Law*, or Law impairing the Obligations of Contracts, or grant any Title of Nobility.

. . . .

ARTICLE II

Section 1. . . . .

[8] Before he enter on the Execution of his Office, he shall take the following Oath or Affirmation: "I do solemnly swear (or affirm) that I will faithfully execute the Office of President of the United States, and will to the best of my Ability, preserve, protect and defend the Constitution of the United States."

Section 2 [1] . . . .

he shall have Power to grant Reprieves and Pardons for Offenses against the United States, except in Cases of Impeachment.

. . . .

Section 3. He shall from time to time give to the Congress Information of the State of the Union, and recommend to their Consideration such Measures as he shall judge necessary and expedient; he may, on extraordinary Occasions, convene both Houses, or either of them, and in Case of Disagreement between them, with Respect to the Time of Adjournment, he may adjourn them to such Time as he shall think proper; he shall receive Ambassadors and other public Ministers; *he shall take Care that the Laws be faithfully executed*, and shall Commission all the officers of the United States.

Section 4. The President, Vice President and all civil Officers of the United States, shall be removed from Office on Impeachment for, and Conviction of, Treason, Bribery, or other high Crimes and Misdemeanors.

ARTICLE III

Section 1. The judicial Power of the United States, shall be vested in one supreme Court, and in such inferior Courts as the Congress may from time to time ordain and establish. The Judges, both of the supreme and inferior Courts, shall hold their Offices during good Behaviour, and shall, at stated Times, receive for their Services a Compensation, which shall not be diminished during their Continuance in Office.

Section 2. [1] *The judicial Power shall extend to all Cases, in Law and Equity, arising under this Constitution, the Laws of the United States, and Treaties made, or which shall be made, under their Authority;*—to all Cases affecting Ambassadors, other public Ministers and Consuls;—to all Cases of admiralty and maritime Jurisdiction;—to Controversies to which the United States shall be a Party;—to Controversies between two or more States;—between a State and Citizens of another State;—between Citizens of different States;—between Citizens of the same State claiming Lands under the Grants of different States, and between a State, or the Citizens thereof, and foreign States, Citizens or Subjects.

[2] In all Cases affecting Ambassadors, other public Ministers and Consuls, and those in which a State shall be a Party, the supreme Court shall have original Jurisdiction. In all the other Cases before mentioned, the supreme Court shall have appellate Jurisdiction, both as to Law and Fact, *with such Exceptions, and under such Regulations as the*

Congress shall make.

[3] The trial of all Crimes, *except in Cases of Impeachment,* shall be by Jury; and such Trial shall be held in the State where the said Crimes shall have been committed; but when not committed within any State, the Trial shall be at such Place or Places as the Congress may by Law have directed.

Section 3. [1] Treason against the United States, shall consist only in levying War against them, or, in adhering to their Enemies, giving them Aid and Comfort. No Person shall be convicted of Treason unless on the Testimony of two Witnesses to the same overt Act, or on Confession in open Court.

. . . .